D0435753

Collective Biographies

GREAT
AMERICAN
BUSINESSWOMEN

Laura S. Jeffrey

ENSLOW PUBLISHERS, INC.

44 Fadem Road   P.O. Box 38
Box 699   Aldershot
Springfield, N.J. 07081   Hants GU12 6BP
U.S.A.   U.K.

Library of Congress Cataloging-in-Publication Data

Jeffrey, Laura S.
    Great American businesswomen / Laura S. Jeffrey.
        p. cm. — (Collective biographies)
    Includes bibliographical references and index.
    ISBN 0-89490-706-9
        1. Women in business—United States—Biography. 2. Women
executives—United States—Biography. I. Title. II. Series.
HC102.5.A2J34   1996
658.4'0092'273—dc20
   [B]   96-1009
                               CIP

Printed in the U.S.A.

10 9 8 7 6 5 4 3 2

Illustration Credits:
BARBIE is a trademark owned by Mattel, Inc. ©1995 Mattel, Inc. All rights
reserved. Used with permission, pp. 36, 42, 44; Courtesy of Alice Rivlin/OMB,
The White House, p. 71; Courtesy of Debbi Fields, pp. 92, 100; Courtesy of
Elaine Garzarelli, pp. 74, 78; Ford Models, Inc., pp. 56, 62; Katharine Graham,
The Washington Post Company, pp. 46, 53; Madam Walker Urban Life Center
Collection, p. 16; National Park Service, Maggie L. Walker National Historic
Site, pp. 8, 14; Photograph by Madam C.J. Walker Collection, Indiana
Historical Society Library, p. 23; Photographs reprinted with the permission of
Harpo, Inc., pp. 82, 87, 89; Radcliffe College, p. 64; Raytheon Aircraft Photo,
pp. 26, 32.

Cover Illustration: Courtesy of Debbi Fields

Contents

Preface 4

1   Maggie L. Walker:
First Female Banker 9

2   Madam C. J. Walker:
African-American Entrepreneur 17

3   Olive Ann Beech:
First Lady of Aviation 27

4   Ruth Handler:
The Creator of Barbie® 37

5   Katharine Graham:
Publishing Powerhouse 47

6   Eileen Ford: A Model Career 57

7   Alice Rivlin:
Adviser to the President 65

8   Elaine Garzarelli:
The Wizard of Wall Street 75

9   Oprah Winfrey:
If She Can Make It 83

10   Debbi Fields:
Sweet Smell, and Taste, of Success . . . 93

Chapter Notes 103

Index 110

Preface

Every day, millions of American women leave their homes and head for jobs. They write newspaper articles or annual reports, or edit books. Perhaps they practice law, fly airplanes, design buildings, or manage money. They may tend to the sick, or teach children.

Some women work because they need the income. For many others, however, working outside the home is as natural as breathing. They enjoy the challenge, excitement, and recognition. Though their days may be exhausting and frustrating, they also are exhilarating and rewarding. These women benefit psychologically as well as financially from working. Through their careers, they offer valuable contributions to society.

This book profiles ten such American women. They stand out from others because they rose to the top of their fields. In the process of achieving their goals, some of them overcame severe disadvantages. Madam C. J. Walker, for example, was born into a very poor family shortly after the Civil War. She had less than $2 to her name when she began creating beauty products for other African-American women. Eventually, she became America's first African-American millionaire.

Almost a century later, an African-American baby grew up to become one of the most recognized television personalities in the world. Her talent for talking—and listening—turned her into a very wealthy woman. Her name? Oprah Winfrey.

Today more than 56 million American women work full time.[1] Of this number, about 6.5 million own their own businesses.[2] Included in the following profiles are some notable female business owners. Olive Ann Beech, for example, formed an aviation company with her husband in 1932. After his death, she ran it successfully for three decades. Ruth Handler founded Mattel toy company with her husband in 1944. After retiring, Handler started another company. This one made artificial breasts for cancer patients.

Another working woman with a family business tie is Katharine Graham. Her father owned *The Washington Post* newspaper. Then her husband ran it for seventeen years. When he died, Graham took over. Under her leadership, the newspaper thrived. It won the Pulitzer Prize for public service for breaking the Watergate story. (In 1972, burglars broke into the headquarters of the Democratic National Committee. Reporting by *Washington Post* reporters revealed that the burglars were linked to President Richard M. Nixon.)

Other business owners discussed in this book include Eileen Ford. She started a modeling agency in 1946. Almost fifty years later, it is one of the largest and most prestigious in the world. Debbi Fields took her love of baking and turned it into a multimillion-dollar cookie company. Her chocolate-chip cookies and other sweet treats are sold in Mrs. Fields stores across the United States and six other countries.

Some women profiled in this book did not start their own companies. However, they rose to leadership positions within their companies. Maggie Walker, for example, worked for a fraternal society in the early 1900s. The organization helped African Americans obtain life insurance. At the time, traditional insurance companies refused to serve African Americans.

Elaine Garzarelli studied the stock market for her employer. She predicted the stock market crash of October 1987 a week before it occurred. Because of this and other accurate forecasts, she became known as the Wizard of Wall Street. Alice Rivlin is another working woman in the financial field. As White House budget director, she advises President Bill Clinton on economic issues.

As the following stories prove, women have made great strides toward equality in the workplace. However, there still may be a long way to go. *Fortune* magazine recently surveyed more than two hundred chief executives of the largest companies in the United States. The poll found that only 16 percent of the executives believed it was "very likely" or "somewhat likely" they would be succeeded by a female in the next ten years. Only 18 percent thought it was "very likely" they would be succeeded by a woman after twenty years. The main reason, the survey found, was discrimination. Many men just cannot imagine women in top leadership positions.[3]

Also, women typically are paid less than men with similar responsibilities and experience. On average, a woman working full time in 1994 earned about seventy-six cents for every dollar earned by a man.[4] Another challenge is juggling a family life with a career. Some working women have been able to find a happy balance between work and home. Others sacrificed marriage, time with children, and other personal interests for their professional lives.

The women introduced on the following pages probably would empathize with their working sisters. They, too, faced discrimination, financial woes, and problems with their personal lives. They persevered, however, and succeeded beyond prediction. In the end, the struggle made the success much more meaningful.

Maggie L. Walker

Maggie L. Walker
First Female Banker

Maggie Lena Walker overcame many hardships to become one of the most important African-American businesswomen in history. Walker was the daughter of a former slave. She grew up poor yet became rich through ingenuity and hard work. She not only bettered her own life but also helped others in the African-American community.

Maggie Walker worked for a fraternal society (a group whose members had common interests and goals). Through this organization, she helped African-Americans obtain life insurance. She also founded the society's newspaper and bank. Maggie was the first female leader—black or white—of a bank in the United States. Today, it is America's oldest continuously operated African-American bank.

Maggie Lena was born on July 15, 1867, in

Richmond, Virginia, two years after the end of the Civil War (1861–1865). Richmond had been left in ruins from the war and was in the process of rebuilding. The city's African Americans were seeking opportunities to distance themselves from slavery.

Maggie was the daughter of Elizabeth Draper, a former slave, and Eccles Cuthbert, a white writer with whom Elizabeth had a brief love affair. In the 1800s, interracial relationships were considered very scandalous. Eccles never denied he fathered Maggie, but he did not play an important role in her life.

Elizabeth Draper worked as a cook for Elizabeth Van Lew, a rich white woman who had been a Union spy during the Civil War. Mrs. Van Lew's butler was William Mitchell, an African American. Elizabeth Draper and William fell in love and were married in 1868. When William became head waiter at a hotel, he moved his new family out of Mrs. Van Lew's mansion and into their own home.

In 1875, William Mitchell was killed in a robbery. His widow had to wash and iron clothes to support her family. Maggie, then eight years old, took on many responsibilities. She delivered the freshly washed laundry to her mother's customers and baby-sat her little brother Johnnie. Meanwhile, she excelled in school.

When Maggie was fourteen years old, she joined the local council of the Independent Order of Saint Luke. The Order of Saint Luke was a national fraternal society for African Americans. It was established in

1867 in Baltimore, Maryland. The organization's goals were similar to those of traditional life-insurance companies. They included collecting dues, paying the medical bills of poor African Americans, and providing burials. At the time, traditional life-insurance companies only served whites.

Maggie graduated from Armstrong Normal and High School in 1883 at the age of sixteen. Then she became a grade-school teacher. Meanwhile, she became more active in Saint Luke. Her initial duties were visiting the sick members and also collecting membership dues. She demonstrated great leadership qualities, however, and quickly captured the attention of national Saint Luke leaders. She became a national deputy and organized local chapters in Virginia and West Virginia.

On September 14, 1886, Maggie married Armstead Walker and became Maggie Lena Walker. Armstead was a building contractor several years her senior. Maggie Walker stopped teaching, but she continued her work for Saint Luke. In 1890 she was elected Right Worthy Grand Chief. This was the highest voluntary office in the organization. That same year, Maggie and Armstead's son, Russell, was born. Another son, Melvin, was born in 1897.

Walker raised her children while continuing to work. In 1895, for example, she organized a drive to recruit children to join the society. Youngsters throughout the South joined local councils to study the Bible, save money, keep clean, and work hard.[1]

In the first year alone, more than one thousand children signed up. Despite Walker's efforts, the national organization was in poor financial condition. Walker soon would become key to the group's survival.

In 1899, Walker became Right Worthy Grand Secretary, the organization's top leadership position. At the time, Saint Luke had about one thousand members and only about $32 in the treasury. The group's bills amounted to $400. Walker had many challenges, but she quickly began turning things around. After her first year in office, the organization's membership doubled. Almost $2,000 was added to the treasury. Walker said:

> To stand still and keep in the same old rut would be a positive crime, and a downright refusal to use these powers, advantages and opportunities which God has given to make our Order the strongest, best, and most beneficial.[2]

In 1902, Walker began publishing a weekly newspaper. The *St. Luke Herald* kept members informed about activities and events. It also publicized the group's successes to the public at large. A year later, Walker established the Saint Luke Penny Savings Bank. Maggie Walker became America's first woman bank president, black or white. "Let us put our money out [to lend] among ourselves, and realize the benefit ourselves," Walker said. "Let us have a bank that will take the nickels and turn them into dollars."[3]

Walker's bank did, indeed, prove to be very

successful. Its president also prospered. In 1904, Walker and her husband purchased a house in an upper-class, African-American neighborhood. It became home to Walker's sons and their families as well. Walker also provided overnight accommodations to friends and business acquaintances. The South was segregated, and few hotels were available to African Americans who needed a place to stay.

In 1908, Walker fell and hurt her knee. It never healed properly, and she began having difficulty walking. This event marked the beginning of a period of personal tragedies. One night in 1915, Walker's son, Russell, mistook Armstead for a burglar and shot him. Russell was overcome with grief and guilt over his father's death. He died eight years later. Walker became wheelchair-bound in 1928.

Despite these misfortunes, Walker thrived professionally. She continued as president of the bank until 1931. The bank remained strong even during the Great Depression (1929–early 1940s). In fact, it loaned Richmond public schools several thousand dollars so that they could continue to operate during those tough economic times.

Eventually the bank merged with two others to become The Consolidated Bank and Trust Company. Today, it is the oldest continuously operated African-American bank in the United States.

Walker also remained active in several civic and women's groups. For example, she helped organize a national organization for African-American women

Maggie L. Walker and her husband, Armstead, purchased this Richmond, Virginia, home in 1904.

in 1930. She also was on the board of directors for the National Association for the Advancement of Colored People (NAACP).

On December 15, 1934, the leader of the Independent Order of Saint Luke died. She was remembered as not only a great community leader but also a nationally respected businessperson. "The passing of Mrs. Maggie L. Walker removes from the scene one of the greatest Negro leaders in America," the *Richmond Times-Dispatch* stated in an editorial.[4]

Through Walker's hard work and guidance, Saint Luke had grown to one hundred thousand members. It had a reserve fund of $100,000. The organization owned a modern brick office building, as well as a press for publishing its newspaper. It also employed African-American women at a time when they were barred from most professional jobs.[5] The newspaper is no longer published.

In 1978, her home that was the scene for so many important family and business gatherings was named a National Historic Site. "The lessons of [Maggie Walker's] life . . . will make one of the most thrilling . . . chapters in the history of Virginia and of our democracy," a reader noted in a letter to the *Richmond News Leader* after Walker's funeral.[6]

Walker herself was humble about her accomplishments. In a speech she said, "If I had my life to live over, I would ask no more than to be able to serve the Saint Luke order faithfully and to the best of my ability, as I have done in the past."[7]

Madam C. J. Walker

Madam C. J. Walker
African-American Entrepreneur

Madam C. J. Walker seemed unlikely to become a businessperson, let alone a millionaire. She was born into a very poor African-American family shortly after the end of the Civil War (1861–1865). Walker married as a teenager, then was widowed only a few years later. She was unable to read or write for much of her life because she was not able to attend school.

Yet Walker was ambitious and determined. With less than $2 to her name, she began creating hair-care products for African-American women. She became very rich. In fact, Walker was the first African-American millionaire. More important, she created job opportunities for thousands of African Americans so they, too, could strive to achieve wealth and success.

Madam C. J. Walker's real name was Sarah Breedlove. She was born on December 23, 1867, in Delta, Louisiana. Sarah spent her early childhood in a tiny, ramshackle cabin on a cotton plantation. Her parents, Owen and Minerva Breedlove, had been slaves there. After they were freed, they continued to work the cotton fields as sharecroppers. Sharecroppers worked for land owners in exchange for a small portion of the crops they harvested. They sold their own crops to earn a meager living. By the time Sarah was five, she was picking cotton along with her brother and sister. She worked long hours under the hot Louisiana sun.

When Sarah was seven years old, her parents contracted yellow fever and died. Sarah's older brother, Alex, moved to Vicksburg, Mississippi, to find work. Sarah stayed in Delta with her older sister, Louvenia. They worked the fields for a few years, but it was very difficult to earn a living. In 1878, the sisters followed their brother to Vicksburg. Sarah lived with Louvenia and Louvenia's husband. Her brother, Alex, eventually left Mississippi and moved to Denver, Colorado.

Louvenia's husband was very cruel to Sarah. The young girl was anxious to escape the abusive household. When she was fourteen years old, she married Moses McWilliams. He was a laborer, and Sarah was a washer. In 1885, Sarah and Moses's daughter, Lelia, was born. Two years later, Moses McWilliams died in a racially motivated killing.

Seeking a better life for herself and her young daughter, Sarah moved to St. Louis, Missouri.

The young widow spent the next eighteen years working as a cook and washer. She did not earn much money, but she was able to save enough to send Lelia to college. Sarah herself was unable to read or write. She also was self-conscious about her hair. It was badly damaged from attempts to straighten it and was falling out. Other African-American women experienced similar problems because of poor health or from using products with harsh chemicals.

One day in 1904, Sarah saw a newspaper picture of Booker T. Washington's wife, Margaret. Washington, a prominent African-American educator, was the founder of Tuskegee Institute in Alabama. Margaret Washington was in St. Louis to attend the World's Fair. She was well-groomed and had beautiful, silky hair. The picture motivated Sarah to try to improve her own appearance.

Sarah began using a hair product made by a St. Louis-based company. She also worked for the company for a short time. Then Sarah experimented with her own solutions. She felt she could make a product that worked better. She asked God to help her devise a formula:

> He answered my prayer, for one night I had a dream, and in that dream a big black man appeared to me and told me what to mix up for my hair.[1]

19

Some of the remedy was grown in Africa, but I sent for it, mixed it, put it on my scalp, and in a few weeks my hair was coming in faster than it had ever fallen out. I tried it on my friends; it helped them. I made up my mind to begin to sell it.[2]

In 1905, Sarah moved to Denver, Colorado. She wanted to be closer to her sister-in-law and four nieces. Her own daughter, Lelia, was away at Knoxville College in Tennessee. When Sarah moved, she left behind a good friend, Charles Joseph Walker. Charles was a salesperson for a local African-American newspaper.

In Denver, Sarah worked first as a cook, then as a washer. In her spare time, she experimented with hair formulas. Eventually, Sarah created three products: Vegetable Shampoo, Wonderful Hair Grower, and Glossine. Meanwhile, she and Charles corresponded frequently. Charles gave Sarah advice on how to market and sell her hair-care products.

Six months after Sarah moved to Denver, Charles joined her there. On January 4, 1906, Sarah became Mrs. C. J. Walker when she and Charles were married. She began calling herself Madam C. J. Walker. She felt "Madam" sounded more dignified than Mrs. She also put this name on her hair-care products.

Madam C. J. Walker began selling her products door-to-door in the city's African-American neighborhoods. She gave free demonstrations of what she called the Walker Method of hair care. First, Walker washed the customer's hair with Vegetable Shampoo. Next, she applied Wonderful Hair Grower. The final step was to apply Glossine, which was a light oil, and then straighten the hair with a heated metal comb she had invented.[3]

Walker advertised her products in the newspaper. She received many mail orders. Her ads included before-and-after shots of her own hair. She also began training other African-American women as sales agents. They received commissions on each product sold.

In 1906, Walker asked her daughter, a recent college graduate, to take over the mail-order operation. With Lelia running the business, Walker went on a trip that lasted more than a year. She traveled throughout the United States to introduce her products.

By 1908, business was booming. Walker decided to move mail-order operations to Pittsburgh, Pennsylvania. This location was more central to other big cities. Here, Walker and Lelia established a school to train African-American women to become Walker agents. She named it Lelia College, after her daughter.

Two years later, in 1910, Walker built a factory in Indianapolis, Indiana, to manufacture her products. In addition to the three products she originally invented, Walker created several other beauty products. At the time, more than five thousand African Americans sold Walker products for commissions. They stressed personal hygiene and self-improvement.

Walker's business was thriving, but her marriage was not. Charles Walker thought it was risky to expand the business beyond Denver. The couple had many disagreements over this. They divorced in 1912. However, Charles Walker continued to work for the company for the rest of his life.

During the next several years, Walker's business continued to grow. She traveled to the Caribbean and West Indies to expand her sales internationally. In 1913, she moved some of her business operations to New York City. Lelia, now calling herself A'Lelia, persuaded her mother to buy a townhouse in the heart of Harlem. This African-American neighborhood was a center of black culture. The women renovated the townhouse into living quarters and a beauty salon. Eventually, salons were established in many other cities.

Walker owned several pieces of property in Los Angeles, California; Chicago, Illinois; and other cities. In 1916, she decided to build a lavish home as an example of what others of her race could achieve. She hired an African-American architect to design a spectacular mansion in Irvington-on-Hudson, New York. The mansion was completed in 1918. At a time when most African-Americans lived in poor, segregated neighborhoods, Walker's "colored woman's palace" attracted much attention.[4]

Madam C. J. Walker stands outside one of her many properties. She later built a spectacular mansion in Irvington-on-Hudson, New York.

Walker lived lavishly, but she also donated a lot of her money. Her nickname was "Lady Bountiful."[5] She gave generously to schools and the National Association for the Advancement of Colored People (NAACP), among other causes. She also set an example of self-improvement by finally learning to read and write.

Despite high blood pressure and kidney problems, the successful entrepreneur maintained a hectic pace. In April 1919, Walker became ill while on a business trip to Saint Louis. She returned to her New York mansion. However, she never recovered. Madam C. J. Walker died on May 25, 1919. She was fifty-one years old.

At the time, more than twenty-five thousand African Americans called themselves Walker agents. Thanks to a determined woman from a deprived background, they made more money than they ever could have imagined. As one graduate of a Walker beauty school wrote to Walker:

> You have opened up a trade for hundreds of colored women to make an honest and profitable living where they make as much in one week as a month's salary would bring from any other position that a colored woman can secure.[6]

A'Lelia Walker took over for her mother until her own death in 1931. The company, known today as Walker Manufacturing, is headquartered in Tuskegee,

Alabama. The legacy of Madam C. J. Walker lives on. As the inspiring woman herself said in 1914:

> I am not merely satisfied in making money for myself, for I am endeavoring to provide employment for . . . the women of my race. I had little or no opportunity when I started out in life. . . . I had to make my own living and my own opportunity! But I made it! That is why I want to say to every Negro woman . . . don't sit down and wait for the opportunities to come. . . . Get up and make them![7]

Olive Ann Beech

3

Olive Ann Beech
First Lady of Aviation

Olive Ann Beech truly was a woman ahead of her time. In an era when most women did not work, she juggled being a wife and mother with running an aviation company with her husband. When he died, Beech took over. She led their company, Beech Aircraft Corporation, for the next thirty years. Under her direction, the company became a leading maker of private airplanes.

Some people wondered whether Olive Ann Beech was simply a lucky woman who married her way into an executive position. But those who know best said Beech Aircraft would never have been a success had Olive Ann Beech not been in charge.[1]

Olive Ann Mellor was born on September 25, 1903, in the farming community of Waverly, Kansas.

Her father, Frank Mellor, was a carpenter. He frequently moved from town to town to take construction jobs. Sometimes his family went with him; other times, they stayed with relatives. Olive Ann's mother, Suzannah Mellor, was a homemaker.

At a very early age, Olive Ann showed an interest in numbers and finance. When she was seven years old, her mother established a bank account for her. By the time Olive Ann was eleven, she was writing checks and paying bills for the family.

In 1917, when Olive Ann was fourteen years old, she and her family moved to Wichita, Kansas. Instead of high school, Olive Ann enrolled in American Business College. She learned stenography, bookkeeping, and spelling. These were skills that traditionally were taught to young women so that they could get secretarial jobs.

Three years later, Olive Ann completed her courses and moved on her own to Augusta, Kansas. There, she became a bookkeeper and office manager for Staley Electrical Company. Olive Ann lived in a boardinghouse with other young working women. Most of them were schoolteachers.

In 1924, Olive Ann's employer died and the office closed. The young woman returned to Wichita and began job-hunting. She learned that a local company, Travel Air Manufacturing, needed a secretary. Travel Air was a leading maker of small airplanes.

Olive Ann knew nothing about airplanes, but

she decided to apply for the job anyway. Travel Air's president and general manager was Walter Beech. He was a former Army Air Corps pilot who was considered a genius at designing and selling airplanes. However, he did not have strong financial skills.[2]

Olive Ann became the only woman on a staff of twelve employees. She also was the only employee who was not a pilot. Yet she quickly learned the business. She recalled:

> When I first started working at Travel Air, I didn't know the empennage [tail assembly] of an airplane from the wing. After a great deal of teasing from the staff . . . I had our chief engineer give me a complete breakdown of an airplane, with the names for the various components marked.[3]

Olive Ann soon impressed Walter Beech with her financial knowledge and hard work. She was promoted to receptionist, then bill collector and paymaster. "Business fascinated me," she recalled. "And it was not difficult to do."[4]

By the late 1920s, Travel Air was the world's leading producer of commercial airplanes. Olive Ann frequently accompanied her boss when he flew in national air races and derbies. They developed a close personal relationship.

In 1929, Walter Beech sold Travel Air to Curtiss-Wright, another aviation company. A year later, on February 24, 1930, Olive Ann Mellor and

Walter Beech were married. She became known as Olive Ann Beech. The couple moved to New York. Walter Beech worked as a vice president of the newly merged aviation company. Olive Ann Beech turned her attentions to homemaking.

After a few years, Walter Beech became bored with his "desk job." He wanted to design and build planes again. Olive Ann Beech also was eager to get back to business. So Walter resigned from Curtiss-Wright, and the couple returned to Wichita. There, in April 1932, they formed Beech Aircraft Corporation. Walter was the company president. Olive Ann was secretary-treasurer and director. She insisted on receiving a paycheck.

The new aviation company was formed during the Great Depression (1929–early 1940s) when many Americans faced great economic hardship. Yet the Beeches plunged enthusiastically into their new endeavor. "The first year of Beechcraft was a lean one. We did not sell an airplane," Olive Ann recalled. "The second year was a little better. We sold one plane for $17,000. Then things started to pick up and they have continued to improve ever since."[5]

Walter Beech's first project was designing a five-seat biplane that had a comfortable yet luxurious interior. This plane, the Model 17, is now considered an aviation classic. Meanwhile, Olive Ann Beech handled the financial side of the company. She also was an important adviser to her husband. It was Olive Ann, for example, who encouraged Walter to hire a woman to fly a Model 17 in the 1936 Bendix Transcontinental Speed Dash. Olive Ann Beech believed a woman pilot would prove a Beech plane could be flown without brute strength.[6] Louise Thaden flew the plane and won the famous cross-country race, setting a new transcontinental speed record for women.

In 1937, Walter and Olive Ann's first daughter, Suzanne, was born. But unlike other women of her era, Olive Ann Beech continued to work. Her role at the company became even more important three years later. In 1940, Walter Beech was hospitalized with encephalitis, which is swelling of the brain. Olive Ann Beech was in the hospital at the same time, giving birth to the couple's second daughter, Mary Lynn.

With Walter in a coma and gravely ill, Olive Ann Beech ran the company from her hospital room. She even called a board of directors meeting around her bed. When she heard that one of her executives was trying to take over Walter's job, she fired the executive and thirteen of his supporters.

Walter Beech returned to work after a year, but he never was quite the same again. Instead, his wife unofficially took over the responsibilities of running the company. "I think I'll get myself a shave," Walter was known to say when problems arose. "Olive Ann can handle this."[7]

Under Olive Ann's direction, Beech became a major supplier of military airplanes during World

Olive Ann Beech and her husband, Walter, inspect one of several assembly lines at the Beech factory in 1941.

War II. In fact, Beech supplied the planes on which 90 percent of American bombardiers and navigators were trained. In 1943, *The New York Times* named Olive Ann Beech as one of the twelve most distinguished women in the United States.

Beech Aircraft's sales were down after World War II. Under Olive Ann Beech's guidance, the company produced corn harvesters, cotton pickers, and washing machines to keep afloat. Meanwhile, Beech engineers worked on new airplane designs.

The aviation side of the business picked up again when the United States entered the Korean War (1950–1953) in June 1950. Five months later, Walter Beech died of a heart attack. His wife became president, chairman of the board, and chief executive of the company. "When Walter Beech died last month, there was no trouble finding someone to fill his job," *Time* magazine reported in December 1950.[8]

During the Korean War, Beech Aircraft supplied the military with many airplanes. In December 1955, the company introduced a new military plane, Model 73. It was the world's smallest jet.

Throughout the 1950s and 1960s, Beech Aircraft prospered. It produced military and commercial airplanes and manufactured parts for other aircraft companies. The company also developed systems for the National Aeronautics and Space Administration (NASA).

On the job, Olive Ann Beech developed a

reputation for being very strict. She also had a clever system to let workers know what kind of mood she was in on a particular day. She flew small flags outside of her office door. A black flag with "Woe" written on it meant the boss was in a bad mood. A royal blue flag with a golden sun and the words "OH HAPPY DAY" indicated that all was well—for the time being.

In 1968, at the age of sixty-five, Olive Ann Beech turned the presidency of Beech over to her nephew, Frank E. Hedrick. She continued as chief executive. At the time, Beech Aircraft was the second largest manufacturer of light aircraft in the United States.

Twelve years later, Olive Ann sold Beech Aircraft to Raytheon Company. Her business had grown from a handful of employees to more than ten thousand workers. Annual sales were more than $900 million. Beech continued as chairman of the board until September 1982.

Olive Ann Beech received many prestigious honors for her life's work. They included the National Aeronautics Association's Wright Brothers Memorial Trophy. She received this annual award in December 1980 "in recognition of significant public service of enduring value to aviation in the United States."[9]

The pioneering working woman was inducted into the Aviation Hall of Fame in July 1981. During her life, she also advised Presidents Dwight

Eisenhower, Lyndon Johnson, and Richard Nixon on aviation issues. When she was not working, she was active in business, cultural, and civic organizations.

Olive Ann Beech died at her home in Wichita, Kansas, on July 6, 1993. She was eighty-nine years old. The woman who came to be known as the First Lady of Aviation was proof of her own belief that women could be successful in any business, as long as they were determined and willing to work hard.

Ruth Handler

Ruth Handler
The Creator of Barbie®

For more than thirty years, generations of children have grown up with Barbie®. The doll not only is a beloved toy, but she is also a billion-dollar-a-year seller. In fact, Barbie® is one of the most successful toys ever manufactured.[1]

Ruth Handler is the businessperson behind Barbie®. She created the doll for Mattel, the company she founded with her husband. Then, after her long and successful career as a toy executive, Handler came up with another winning idea. She created a company to make artificial breasts for breast-cancer patients.

Ruth Mosko was born on November 4, 1916, in Denver, Colorado. She was the youngest of ten children of Polish immigrants. Her father, Jacob Mosko, was a blacksmith. Her mother, Ida Mosko, was a homemaker.

When Ruth was six months old, her mother had gallbladder surgery. Ruth went to live with her sister Sarah, who was twenty years old. Ida Mosko recovered, but her health was not good. Sarah, who could not have children of her own, raised Ruth to adulthood.

Sarah and her husband, Louie, were shopkeepers. They owned a drugstore and then a liquor store. By the time Ruth was ten, she was helping out at the businesses after school. Later, she also worked as a secretary for her brother Joe, a lawyer. These early experiences led Ruth to believe it was normal—even fun—for women to work outside the home. "[I] always had a compulsion to work," she said.[2]

When Ruth was sixteen, she met Elliot Handler at a neighborhood carnival. They began dating, even though Sarah discouraged the relationship. "My family didn't want me to marry Elliot because they thought he would always be a starving artist," Ruth recalled.[3]

Ruth graduated from high school in 1934. Then she enrolled at the University of Denver in Colorado to study prelaw. Elliot, who also graduated from high school that year, went to a Denver art school. They continued to date, much to Sarah's dismay.

The summer after Ruth's sophomore year in college, she vacationed with a friend in Los Angeles, California. Ruth liked the city so much she decided to stay. She found a job as a secretary at Paramount Studios. Sarah, eager for Ruth and Elliot to be apart, encouraged the move.

A few months later, however, Elliot also moved to Los Angeles. He designed lighting fixtures to earn a living and started dating Ruth again. After a year, Sarah persuaded Ruth to move back to Denver. Again, Elliot followed her. This time, he convinced Sarah that he loved Ruth and would be a good husband.

Finally, with her family's approval, Ruth Mosko and Elliot Handler were married on June 26, 1938. The newlyweds spent their honeymoon driving back to Los Angeles to make a home for themselves. Ruth got her old job back with Paramount.

Ruth and Elliot Handler's first business venture began shortly after they were married. Elliot made bookends, trays, candleholders, lamps, and tables to furnish their apartment. Ruth noticed how well they were made. She asked him, "Why don't we try selling the stuff?"[4]

In her spare time, Handler took her husband's pieces to various shops. She persuaded the owners to place orders. Next, Elliot created costume jewelry out of scraps of plastic. Again, Ruth Handler marketed the pieces. She drummed up so many orders that eventually Elliot took on four business partners to handle the work.

Under her doctor's orders, Ruth stopped working at Paramount when she became pregnant.

Elliot and Ruth's daughter, Barbara, was born in May 1941. Their son, Ken, was born three years later. Ruth enjoyed being a mother, but Elliot needed her help with a new venture. He and one of his business partners, Harold "Matt" Matson, had decided to leave their other two partners and start a new company. They were unsure what kinds of items their new company should produce.

Ruth Handler suggested they start by manufacturing picture frames. She even found a company to place a big order. Working out of an abandoned garage, Matson and Elliot Handler began turning out the frames. They combined their names and called their new company Mattel. Ruth recalled years later:

> It never even occurred to me that some part of "Ruth," by all rights, belonged in the name, since it was my idea to start with picture frames and I brought in that first big order. But this was 1944, and just as a woman got her identity through her husband in her personal life—you were Mrs. John Smith, not Sally Smith—should it not be so in business?[5]

After the picture frames, Mattel began manufacturing dollhouse furniture. Again, Ruth Handler found buyers. Next, the company created plastic ukeleles and toy pianos. These items established Mattel as a major toy company.

In 1947, Matson sold his share of the toy company to Ruth's sister, Sarah, and her husband,

Louis. Mattel was now a family business, with Elliot Handler as president and Ruth Handler the enthusiastic sales manager.

Mattel began manufacturing a line of musical toys, including music boxes and books. By 1951, the company had grown to six hundred employees and had moved into a sixty-thousand-square-foot building. A year later, Mattel had sold more than 20 million music boxes. Ruth and Elliot Handler, each thirty-five years old, were being called the "whiz kids of the toy trade."[6]

In 1955, Mattel's toy guns became big sellers. That year, Ruth came up with the idea to advertise toys on television. This transformed Mattel from a profitable business into a corporate giant.[7]

Then came Barbie®. From watching her daughter Barbara at play, Ruth Handler realized that girls needed dolls that allowed them to pretend they were something other than mommies. However, the only dolls on the market were baby dolls.

"The whole philosophy of Barbie® was that through the doll, a girl could be anything she wanted to be," Ruth said.[8]

Ruth asked Mattel's design staff to create an eleven-inch doll to her specifications. The doll was called Barbie®, after the Handlers' daughter. A fashion designer was hired to create a wardrobe for the new doll.

Barbie the Teen-Age Fashion Model® was introduced in 1959. She was followed by Ken®, who was

41

Among the many famous dolls created by Ruth Handler and Mattel, Inc. was Teacher Barbie®.

named after the Handlers' son. Next came Midge®, Skipper®, and a host of other dolls and accessories. In 1993, the typical American girl between the ages of three and ten owned an average of eight Barbie® dolls. Sales that year were more than $1 billion.[9]

Mattel had many other successes, including the Chatty Cathy® doll, Hot Wheels® cars, and See 'N Say® toys. Elliot Handler focused on product development, while Ruth Handler became president of Mattel. She also received many honors, including being named to the Toy Industry Hall of Fame by the Toy Manufacturers of America.

Despite her successes, Handler encountered prejudice because of her gender. "I can reel off anecdote after anecdote about how it was made abundantly clear to me in the business world that I was a fluke, a quirk, not normal," she said.[10]

In June 1970, tragedy struck. Handler was diagnosed with breast cancer. She underwent a mastectomy. At the same time, Mattel began having financial and legal problems. Handler's personal and professional troubles became overwhelming.

Characteristically, she bounced back. Unsatisfied with the artificial breasts that were on the market, she decided that she could do better. She and her husband retired from Mattel in 1975. A year later, Handler formed a new company, called Nearly Me, to manufacture more realistic and affordable breast prostheses.

The entrepreneur spent the next several years

Super Power Barbie® was another of Ruth Handler and
Mattel, Inc.'s creations.

building her new company. She traveled to department stores across the country, introducing her product and instructing workers about fittings. Sales flourished, and her artificial breasts were called "the Cadillac of the business."[11]

In 1989, Handler had her other breast removed as a precaution against getting cancer again. Two years later, she sold Nearly Me.

Today, Handler reflects on her accomplishments with pride and satisfaction. She also believes she did a good job balancing motherhood with a career. For example, she and Elliot left work every day at 5:30 P.M. so they could have dinner with their children. They also made it a rule never to talk about business until Barbara and Ken were in bed. Saturdays were reserved for family shopping trips or going to the movies.

When Handler hears talk about "the glass ceiling," she reminds women that in her day, the ceiling was concrete. ("Glass ceiling" is an expression that means women can see better job opportunities, but they are prevented from achieving them.)

Handler also advises women to have faith in themselves. "It took me years to realize that being female actually gave me strength," she said. "Women are more in touch with their feelings, which gives them certain intuitive sensitivities to other people."[12]

Katharine Graham

5

Katharine Graham
Publishing Powerhouse

For much of her life, Katharine "Kay" Graham stood one step away from the spotlight. She grew up as the daughter of Agnes and Eugene Meyer, two very wealthy and influential people. Then she married Philip Graham. He was an intelligent and popular man who became publisher of *The Washington Post* newspaper. In the company of these powerful and famous people, Graham felt like a "nobody."[1]

When her husband died, however, Kay Graham became the center of attention. Despite her lack of self-confidence, she took over as the *Washington Post* publisher. Under her leadership, the newspaper thrived. Graham became known as a very powerful woman.[2]

Katharine Meyer was born on June 16, 1917, in New York City. She was the fourth of five children of Eugene and Agnes Meyer. Eugene Meyer had made a fortune as a Wall Street investment banker. He also served as a government administrator under five United States Presidents. Agnes Meyer was an author, lecturer, and political activist.

The Meyer family spent winters in their Washington, D.C., mansion. Politicians, artists, doctors, musicians, and other well-known people visited often. Summers were spent on the family farm in upstate New York.

Although Kay's life was privileged, it also was lonely. She and her siblings spent most of their time in the care of servants. They also were overwhelmed by their parents' achievements. A relative recalled years later:

> [They] felt they were neglected or squashed or held up to some unattainable standard. They were expected to be beautiful and glamorous and perfect. And they were taught that they were failures if they weren't.[3]

Kay attended Madeira, an exclusive private school outside of Washington. She played field hockey and lacrosse and was editor of the student newspaper. In 1933, the year before Kay graduated, her father purchased *The Washington Post* at a bankruptcy sale. "It was the weakest of five papers in Washington then, and no one expected it to survive," Kay recalled.[4] At the time, her father said he found it "mentally, morally, physically and in every other way bankrupt."[5]

In 1934, Kay enrolled at Vassar College in Poughkeepsie, New York. She wrote for the campus newspaper and became involved in political activities. After her sophomore year, Kay transferred to the University of Chicago in Illinois. During her summer vacations, she worked at the *Post*. Her father invested millions of dollars in the newspaper. He replaced broken-down presses and other equipment, raised workers' salaries, and hired bright young college graduates as reporters. Eugene Meyer wanted to make the newspaper respectable as well as profitable.

Kay graduated from the University of Chicago with a history degree in 1938. She moved to California to become a reporter for the *San Francisco News*. After a year, she returned to Washington. Eugene Meyer wanted his daughter to work at the *Post* and learn all about the newspaper. He believed that she would one day take over as publisher. Of all the Meyer children, Kay seemed the most interested and qualified.[6]

Kay wrote articles, attended editorial meetings, and worked in the advertising and circulation departments. She also wrote headlines and learned how to assemble pages. However, her career was cut short when she met Philip Graham. He was a law clerk for a Supreme Court Justice. Kay described him as "a marvelous, fantastic, magical . . . genius."[7] The couple fell in love and were married on June 5, 1940.

The United States entered World War II in December 1941. The following year, Phil Graham enlisted in the Army Air Corps. Kay Graham accompanied her husband as he was transferred to various Army posts in the United States. The couple had a daughter, Elizabeth (called Lally), in 1944. Their son, Donald, was born in 1945. When Phil was shipped overseas, Kay Graham returned to Washington with their children. She occasionally wrote columns for her father's newspaper. She also answered phones in the *Post*'s complaint department.

World War II ended in 1945, and Phil Graham left the Army. He considered moving his family to his home state of Florida to continue his law career. However, Eugene Meyer persuaded his son-in-law to work at the newspaper. In January 1946, Phil Graham was named assistant to the publisher. Six months later, he became publisher of *The Washington Post*. Graham was happy that her husband took the job that once might have been hers. "[I] was honestly convinced that women were inferior to men," she recalled.[8]

Phil Graham spent the next seventeen years building the *Post* empire. He purchased the *Times Herald*, a competitive Washington newspaper. With this move, the *Post* boosted its advertising and circulation figures. He also bought *Newsweek* magazine, several radio and television stations, and a news service, among other properties.

The energetic man also developed a national reporting bureau for his newspaper and devoted more money and staff to the editorial page. Also, a new company headquarters was built. It featured color presses and air-conditioning.

Meanwhile, Kay Graham raised the couple's four children. Sons William and Stephen were born in 1948 and 1953, respectively. She said:

> I was the kind of wife that women liberationists talk about. I was a second-class citizen and my role was to keep Phil happy, peaceful, calm and functioning, and the children the same. I guess because I'd been brought up by nurses and governesses and never saw my parents, I compensated by spending as much time as I could with my children. [Phil] was so glamorous that I was perfectly happy just to clean up after him.[9]

Yet all was not well in the Graham household. Phil had been diagnosed with manic depression. This is a mental illness characterized by wide mood swings. He could not overcome the feelings of hopelessness he often experienced. On August 3, 1963, Phil Graham killed himself.

At the age of forty-six, Kay Graham found herself as publisher of the *Post*. It was the job she seemed destined to fill. In the beginning, however, she did not plan on actually being in charge. Graham recalled:

> I started out with the idea that I should learn enough to be knowledgeable and intelligent, should I ultimately have to make any important decisions. It never occurred to me that I would manage anything. . . . I assumed everything would go on much as before, with the men [who were] already running things continuing to do what they were doing.[10]

But as Graham gained confidence in herself, she discovered she not only enjoyed leading, but she was good at it. She followed her father's three basic rules of business: Know everything there is to know, work harder than anybody else, and be absolutely honest.[11]

The new publisher also surrounded herself with loyal, competent colleagues. In perhaps her wisest hiring decision, she named Benjamin Bradlee as managing editor in 1965. Under his direction, the *Post* built a staff of top reporters and editors. The paper gained worldwide acclaim for lively, detailed reporting.

Kay Graham became known as a publisher who shared credit for successes. She also allowed her editors and reporters to make their own decisions—with her final approval. In 1971, Graham published the "Pentagon Papers." This was a top-secret government study revealing America's mistakes in Vietnam. Government officials had argued against

Katharine Graham is a publisher known as someone who shares credit for successes.

the publication, saying it would harm national security.

Two years later, reporters Bob Woodward and Carl Bernstein pursued the Watergate story with Graham's encouragement. The *Post*'s reporting of the politically motivated burglary and cover-up caused President Richard Nixon to resign. In 1973, *The Washington Post* was awarded the Pulitzer Prize for Meritorious Public Service for its Watergate coverage. Altogether, the newspaper has won almost thirty of the prestigious awards for outstanding work. Graham has said:

> The journalist's role is to offer a tough-minded appraisal of what things really look like, what's really ailing the world—and the people in it—and why. It provides the only sensible basis on which we can form our opinions, elect our leaders, and shape our policies.[12]

As she grew older, Graham began turning over some of her duties to her son Donald. He became publisher of the *Post* in 1979 and chief executive officer in 1991. Graham herself continues as chairman of The Washington Post Company's executive committee.

Today, *The Washington Post* and *Newsweek* magazine are considered two of the most important national publications. Kay Graham's company is a financial success, and she is one of the richest women in the world. She also has been named in several polls as one of the most admired and influential American women.

But while Graham recognizes her accomplishments, she does not care to be called a powerful woman. "That's a sexist remark and I really dislike it," she said. "That makes me feel like a lady weightlifter."[13]

Eileen Ford

6

Eileen Ford
A Model Career

No one can spot a potential model faster than Eileen Ford. Ford founded one of the largest and most successful modeling agencies of all time. While her husband handled the business side, Ford scouted for new talent. She represented Jean Shrimpton and Suzy Parker, two of the first "supermodels." Other Ford models included Jane Fonda, Ali McGraw, Lauren Hutton, Cheryl Tiegs, Candice Bergen, Christie Brinkley, and Brooke Shields.

According to Ford, a successful model is one who is beautiful on the inside, too. "Today, models must be nice," she said. "People just won't put up with temperament any longer. All my models are nice or they wouldn't be my models."[1] She added, "And no one will put up with dummies, either."[2]

Eileen Otte was born on March 25, 1922, in

New York City. She grew up in Great Neck, New York, with her parents, Loretta and Nathaniel Otte, and three brothers. Her parents operated a business that rated the credit of large corporations. They made a good living and showered their children with material things. Eileen recalled years later:

> I had everything it took to make me . . . happy. I had reasonable marks, nice clothes and a car, a home where I could give a party every week, plenty of boyfriends. I didn't stay out later than I was allowed, and I didn't come home with poor grades. I didn't feel misunderstood. . . . I just respected [my parents], and for that reason I was pretty obedient.[3]

"One thing is sure, I didn't have any desire to work or have a career," Eileen added. "I was horrified at the thought my mother might force me to go to college. She eventually did."[4]

Loretta Otte, a former model, wanted Eileen to become a lawyer.[5] So her daughter enrolled in Barnard College after graduating from high school in 1939. Eileen spent her summer vacations modeling. She graduated in 1943 with a degree in psychology.

Eileen Otte intended to continue on to law school. However, she became sidetracked by fashion-related jobs. First she worked as a photographers' stylist. Then she was a fashion reporter. Eileen enjoyed the glamour and excitement of the industry.

In August 1944, Eileen met Jerry Ford. He was a

college football player two years younger than she was. The couple fell in love, and Jerry decided to leave college. Eileen Otte and Jerry Ford were married three months after they met, on November 20, 1944. Eileen Ford said:

> I decided to elope because I knew if I didn't right then, I would never marry him. I knew my parents would say no. They would have wanted me to marry someone who'd finished college, which Jerry hadn't—someone who had a chauffeur and a governess when he was a kid.[6]

Two years after they were married, Eileen Ford became pregnant. Jerry was working for Eileen's father, but money was tight. To earn extra cash, Eileen began handling bookings for two model friends. At the time, the modeling business was not very organized. Models were expected to set and collect their own fees. The agency was responsible for finding the model work, but her best interests often were not considered.

Eileen Ford took a personal interest in the careers of her models. She negotiated favorable deals with photographers and advertising agencies. Her friends appreciated the service and recommended Ford to other models.

Soon, more models came knocking on Ford's door. When the Fords' daughter, Jamie, was born in 1947, Ford was handling bookings for eight models.

A year later, Ford was the agent for thirty-four fashion models. Jerry, who had been attending business school on top of working, decided to quit his job. He went into business with his wife. On a typical day, Eileen and Jerry Ford spent up to 11 hours at work, making 275 phone calls from the 7 phones in their office.[7]

The Fords later had three more children. Their son, Bill, was born in 1952. Daughters Katie and Lacey were born in 1955 and 1957, respectively. As the Ford family grew, so did the agency. Models appreciated Eileen Ford's motherly touches. She offered them snacks between assignments and helped them prepare for photo shoots. She offered advice on skin and hair problems. Eileen Ford also refused to let her models pose for advertisements that she felt were undignified.

The Fords also established business practices that became standard in the fashion industry. They paid their models weekly. Then they collected money from the photographers and advertising agencies who hired the women.

The Fords offered new models temporary shelter in their New York City town house or country home. The models were treated as though they were family and were expected to help out with household chores. "I have models around me all the time," Ford said. "They live with us, eat with us, stay in our home. I have a responsibility to the girls, whose careers I'm guiding."[8]

Ford also made sure her models lived up to high moral standards. Those who went out too often or stayed out too late were reprimanded. If they did not change their ways, they were dropped from the agency and sent home.

Eileen and Jerry Ford also implemented a standard 20 percent commission that other modeling agencies soon adopted. The model paid 10 percent of what she earned from each assignment. The client paid the other 10 percent. Fees were set for each type of work, such as magazine ads and catalog layouts. Cancellation and fitting fees were established.

Jerry Ford concentrated on the financial side of the business. Eileen Ford's job was to find young women whom she could mold into Ford models. Each year she made several trips throughout the United States and Europe. She also culled through thousands of photos that were sent to her and met aspiring models who showed up at her agency. "The beautiful woman is the one who really knows herself—her face, her body, everything—and she makes the most of everything she's got," Ford said.[9]

Ford looked for faces that photographed well. The specific physical qualities she sought were wide-set eyes, a straight nose, and a long neck. "It's the most difficult thing to tell a girl she's not pretty enough to be a model," Ford said. "You're dealing with a girl's ego, the most tender part of her, and if you hurt that, you can really do serious damage."[10]

Today, Ford is considered an expert in the beauty industry. She has written a syndicated newspaper column and several books about modeling.

Eileen Ford and her husband, Jerry, founded Ford Models, Inc. While Jerry Ford concentrated on the financial side of the business, Eileen Ford's job was to find new models.

Two of her grown children now work for her. Her agency represents hundreds of women. The Ford agency also represents male models as well as child models.

Though Ford is in her seventies, she continues to search for new talent. She said:

> There are two words in the modeling business: bones and body, body and bones. A girl has to have plenty of both to make it. She also needs something else, something that separates a beautiful girl from a great model. I call that something the "X-factor."[11]
>
> A girl who doesn't see herself with a potential of being beautiful can't be a model. The true basis of the successful model is that she believes. That's the first part of my job. The next part is to keep her from believing it so much that it carries her away.[12]

Perhaps surprisingly, Eileen Ford is glad her own daughters did not pursue modeling careers. She also thinks it would be wise for models to keep in mind the temporary nature of the career:

> Because when it's over, you [might] have nothing. I don't mean financially, but inside. It's a temporary career and models are very young when they start and their education suffers. And then in a few years you have nothing to do and you're just an old leftover model. And there's nothing in the world worse than that.[13]

Alice Rivlin

7

Alice Rivlin

Adviser to the President

Outspoken economist Alice M. Rivlin spent much of her career in public service. As a result, she often was at the center of political controversy. During her eight years as head of the Congressional Budget Office, she examined the federal budget and national economy. She also studied the true costs of programs proposed by politicians. Many lawmakers did not appreciate her sometimes harsh, albeit accurate, reports. Currently, Rivlin is President Bill Clinton's budget director.

Alice Mitchell was born on March 4, 1931, in Philadelphia, Pennsylvania. Her mother, Georgianna Mitchell, was a homemaker. Her father, Allan Mitchell, was a college professor. After Alice was born, her father received an offer to teach nuclear physics at the University of Indiana. The Mitchell family moved to Bloomington, Indiana, where Alice grew up.

Alice graduated from high school in 1948. Then she enrolled at Bryn Mawr College in Bryn Mawr, Pennsylvania. Originally, she intended to study history. A summer course changed her mind. "I switched to economics because it seemed more definite and, I think, more useful," she recalled.[1]

Economists determine the most efficient ways to use a nation's resources. They recommend ways to pay for needs such as food, clothing, and shelter. Alice felt a career in economics would be an exciting and worthwhile way to earn a living.

Alice graduated from Bryn Mawr with honors in 1952. In 1955, she earned a master's degree in economics from Radcliffe College in Cambridge, Massachusetts. Three years later, she earned a doctoral degree in economics. Meanwhile, Alice met Lewis A. Rivlin, a lawyer from Washington, D.C. The couple was married in 1955. They made the nation's capital their home.

Alice and Lewis Rivlin eventually had three children. Unlike many other women of her era, Alice Rivlin was not content to be a homemaker. Instead, she pursued a career. "There was definite discrimination [in the workplace]," Rivlin recalled. "But in retrospect, we put up with more than we should have. It was part of the game."[2]

In 1957, Rivlin went to work at the Brookings Institution in Washington, D.C. This private think tank organization researched social issues. It was considered a liberal institution. While at Brookings, Rivlin wrote several books and articles on economics. Her work gained the attention of prominent lawmakers. She was asked to serve as a consultant to the House Committee on Education and Labor during 1961 and 1962. Then, from 1964 until 1966, she advised the secretary of the United States Treasury.

In 1966, Rivlin left Brookings to join President Lyndon B. Johnson's newly created Department of Health, Education and Welfare (HEW). This governmental agency was in charge of programs to promote public welfare. Its name was changed to the Department of Health and Human Services in 1979, when a separate Department of Education was created.

Rivlin was HEW's deputy assistant for program coordination until 1968. She performed so admirably that Johnson promoted her to assistant secretary for planning and evaluation. She worked in this job until 1969, after Richard M. Nixon became President. The new President wanted to appoint his own people to government positions. Rivlin returned to Brookings.

Rivlin continued to analyze economic issues and to publish her findings. One of her most impressive works was a three-volume set. It analyzed President Nixon's budgets of 1971, 1972, and 1973.

In July 1974, Congress established the Congressional Budget Office (CBO). Its mission was to help Congress analyze the cost of legislation that had passed or was being considered. It also was tasked with making economic forecasts for Congress and analyzing alternatives to federal programs. The CBO was to be a nonpartisan organization—neither Democratic nor Republican. Rivlin, who was well-known through her writing and previous government experience, was appointed to a four-year term as director. She was sworn in as the CBO's first director on February 24, 1975.

"When I was first approached about this job, I asked my friend . . . if I'd be crazy to take it," Rivlin recalled. "He said, 'Crazy? I think you'd be insane!'"[3] Rivlin, a Democrat, soon found out what he meant. Republican lawmakers questioned whether her findings were neutral. Public statements she made about the CBO's findings sometimes were at odds with what politicians of both parties said. "It was an often hostile environment," she recalled.[4]

By the end of the 1970s, however, Rivlin and the CBO proved to be a success. "Before the CBO, we just did not have the figures to work with," said Karen Williams, then chief counsel of the Senate Budget Committee. "Now CBO studies on defense issues have allowed us to take a really good look at costs. The same goes for proposed food-stamp and Social Security reform."[5]

Also, Rivlin showed she could act without taking sides. She said in 1977:

> We're operating in an intensely political atmosphere. There's bound to be some hostility to our findings. Before this year, it was Republican programs we were analyzing and it was Republicans who didn't like it. Now it's the Democrats. They're still a bit sensitive.[6]

While Rivlin was succeeding on the job, her home life was unhappy. Career pressures and other factors contributed to the downfall of her marriage. Alice and her husband, Lewis, divorced in 1977.

With President Jimmy Carter in office, Rivlin was appointed to her second term as CBO director. It expired in 1983. Then she returned to the Brookings Institution as director of economic studies. She remained there for four years. During this period, Rivlin's expertise was rewarded, as well as in demand. In 1983, she received a MacArthur Foundation fellowship. This prestigious award is given to those who are leaders in their field. Fellowship winners do not apply; nominators for the foundation search for worthy individuals. Fellowship winners are awarded anywhere from $30,000 to $75,000 annually, for five years. They may do whatever they wish with the money. Many use it to continue their work.

Rivlin wrote about economic issues. She also publicly expressed some of her concerns. "The country ought to be in the best shape it has been in for years," she said in 1984. "We ought to have low interest rates and low deficits, and instead we have high interest rates and high deficits. Now that is a really dumb choice." She added, "We ought to aim for a surplus in the federal budget; we ought not just to narrow the deficit."[7]

Rivlin also was a visiting professor at the Kennedy School of Government at Harvard University. In 1989, she led a commission to help the nation's capital overcome budget deficits.

In 1992, Rivlin wrote *Reviving the American Dream.* Her book focused on how the federal government and individual states should divide responsibilities. Her plan, which *Fortune* magazine called "thoughtful and timely,"[8] would enable the federal budget to be reduced by $75 billion. Rivlin said:

> My proposal isn't liberal or conservative—it's both. I'm concerned with improving public services, not with getting the federal government out of everything. It's a managerial question, and right now there are just too many things for the federal government to manage.[9]

In 1993, Rivlin became President Bill Clinton's deputy director of the White House Office of Management and Budget (OMB). The next year, in

In 1994, Alice Rivlin became deputy director of the White House Office of Management and Budget (OMB).

October 1994, she became director of OMB. Rivlin soon found herself in another controversy. She wrote a memo suggesting possible ways to reduce the federal deficit. (A deficit occurs in the federal budget when money spent on programs and agencies exceeds federal revenues from taxes and other sources.)

Rivlin's memo mentioned touchy issues such as tax increases and cuts in Social Security and Medicare benefits. The memo was leaked and reprinted in *The Washington Post* newspaper. An uproar ensued. The President distanced himself from Rivlin and her ideas. Some lawmakers even suggested that she resign.

Yet Rivlin survived the latest storm. She noted that she was presenting ideas, not making firm recommendations. Her candor even won public praise. "Poor Alice Rivlin," wrote Michael Kramer in *Time* magazine. "She told the truth and is getting burned for it."[10]

Rivlin leads a busy, important life. When controversy arises—as it still does—she remembers something she said during the difficult days at the CBO. "Nobody ever said that democracy was easy," she declared in 1979. "They only said that it was better than any other form of government."[11]

When she is not working, Rivlin walks, hikes, and reads novels. She also speaks about her career field. Economists, she says, "show what has to be given up to achieve alternative policy objectives. . . . They show what the costs are of what the policymaker wants to do." She adds that the role of the economist is "to help make the choices clearer, to show what might happen, and to provide alternative thinking."[12]

For those who think they, too, may want to become an economist, Alice Rivlin has this to say:

> Get the best training you can get. That means more math and more computer science now than in my day. Go to a good graduate school. Then just start working on things that are really interesting to you.[13]

Elaine Garzarelli

8

Elaine Garzarelli
The Wizard of Wall Street

Does Elaine Garzarelli have a crystal ball? Sometimes it certainly seems so. Garzarelli was one of a few financial analysts who accurately predicted the stock market crash of October 1987. Investors who followed her advice did not lose their money. Garzarelli also made other stock market predictions that came true. She became a media celebrity.

Yet while Garzarelli savored success, she also experienced dissatisfaction. The Wall Street Guru, as she was called, left her prestigious job in 1994 and started her own company to research and analyze the stock market.

Elaine Marie Garzarelli was born on October 13, 1952, in Springfield, Pennsylvania, a suburb of Philadelphia. Her father, Ralph, was a loan officer who worked his way up to executive vice president of a bank. Her mother, Ida, was a homemaker.

Elaine had two brothers, one older and one younger. When the Garzarelli children were growing up, their mother stressed hard work and winning. During the summers, she hung a "Do Not Disturb" sign on the front door of the family's home so the children could read and study uninterrupted.

Elaine and her older brother, Robert, often competed for better grades. Together, they played chess and experimented with electricity and physics sets. At the same time, Elaine enjoyed dancing. "I stood out in school as being wilder than most," Elaine recalled. "But on the other hand, I had very good grades."[1]

After Elaine graduated from high school, she attended Drexel University in Philadelphia, Pennsylvania. She started out studying chemical engineering. However, an introductory course in economics convinced her that she should switch majors. "It just clicked; I loved it," she recalled.[2] Eventually, Elaine earned both bachelor's and master's degrees in economics from Drexel.

While Garzarelli was still in college, she began working part-time at a Philadelphia investment firm called Drexel Harriman Ripley. Her first day on the job, the firm's chief economist, Roy E. Moor, noticed the bright new hire. Moor gave her a challenge: Figure out a system for predicting when stocks might rise or fall. (Stocks are pieces of paper that prove someone owns a share in a corporation.) Investors who buy stocks hope to sell them in the future at a higher price and, thus, make money. The company's performance is one factor that determines the stock price. There are many other factors, however.

On her assignment, Garzarelli finally came up with a combination of thirteen economic indicators. She assigned different weights to these. With this secret mathematical formula she devised, Garzarelli began predicting general trends of the stock market.

In 1971, Garzarelli followed Moor when he went to work for another investment firm in Philadelphia called A. G. Becker Paribas, and continued her market-prediction activities. Garzarelli worked hard. After eleven years, she became the firm's first female managing director. She began attracting national attention when she appeared on television business programs to discuss her market predictions.

In 1984, after A. G. Becker merged with another firm, Garzarelli joined Shearson Lehman Brothers. That same year, she was named the top Wall Street analyst in a poll conducted by *Institutional Investor* magazine. Her name would stay in the top spot for the next ten years.

Garzarelli enjoyed her success, but it came at a price. During this period, she was married and divorced twice. She prefers not to discuss these events. "[Elaine] is a part of that transitional generation of women who wanted careers," said her friend Pamela Maraldo. "The men who grew up when we did weren't sympathetic to that."[3]

Elaine Garzarelli at work in her office. In 1984, she was named the top Wall Street analyst in a *Institutional Investor* poll.

Garzarelli also experienced other losses in her life. Her beloved brother, Robert, was killed in a car crash in 1977. Two years later, her father died of a heart attack.

In the early 1980s, the stock market had risen dramatically. Yet by the summer of 1987, Garzarelli began seeing indications that the stock market would fall. She was one of only a few analysts who predicted such an event.

On October 12, 1987, Garzarelli appeared on CNN's *Moneyline*. She said that based on her indicators, she feared the market was on the brink of a catastrophe.[4] One week later, the stock market plunged 508 points. Thousands of investors lost money; some were even wiped out. October 19 came to be known as Black Monday. Even though Garzarelli had been expecting trouble, the market collapse was upsetting. She said:

> I felt as if someone in my family had gotten terribly sick. This is the most uncertain time of my whole career. For me to come up with any [investment] conclusions at all, I had to spend days and nights doing research on prior crashes.[5]

A few years later, Garzarelli made another impressive prediction. In August 1990, during the Persian Gulf crisis, the majority of analysts were predicting the stock market would fall. Garzarelli, however, forecast a bull market. (This is a term for higher stock prices.) Sure enough, prices rose.

For the next several years, Garzarelli accurately

predicted virtually every major move of the stock market.[6] She became a vice president at Shearson, with an annual salary exceeding more than a million dollars. She had twenty-four hundred clients in the United States and about four hundred overseas. Their investments ranged from $100 million to $60 billion each.[7]

Garzarelli became a celebrity. She stood out not only for her stock smarts but also for her individuality. She preferred to research and write her market analyses in her apartment rather than the firm's office building. Garzarelli also favored flashy clothes over the Wall Street uniform of dark business suits. She said in 1988:

> Cosmo [*Cosmopolitan* magazine] called. Television stations. Foreign magazines. I'm single . . . so I'd get marriage proposals. People would call all the time wanting to know what the market was going to do the next day—which was ridiculous! There was so much going on, it took me four months to do my next report.[8]

In 1993, Garzarelli appeared in a television commercial for No Nonsense® pantyhose. The advertising campaign featured women who were leaders in their field. That same year, Shearson merged with another investment company, Smith Barney. The national economy was faltering, and it was a trying time for Wall Street firms. Many were merging with other companies or were closing altogether. As a result, thousands of workers lost their jobs.

In 1994, Garzarelli became one of the unemployed. Shearson announced it could no longer afford her high salary.[9] Also, the mutual fund she managed was not performing to expectations. With the mutual fund, she chose specific stocks for her clients that she felt would perform well.

Garzarelli was embarrassed and angered. "It was all over the front page of every newspaper," she recalled. "It broke my heart."[10] She moved to Boca Raton, Florida, intending to retire. However, her love of the stock market lured her back to work. "I tried [retirement] for a couple of months," she said. "Then I said . . . 'I can't stand it. I've got to have a purpose.'"[11]

From her luxurious Florida home, the analyst started her own firm, Garzarelli Capital. Today she continues to track the stock market and predict its highs and lows. Each month she writes a fifty-page report for about five hundred clients. Then she travels across the country as well as overseas to confer with them.

As a woman in a field dominated by men, Garzarelli has encountered discrimination and sexism. She also has been criticized by other women for her outspokenness and flashy style. "Men stab me in the front," she has said. "The women stab me in the back."[12]

Elaine Garzarelli enjoys her career. One day, however, she wants to concentrate more on her personal life. She may even try to adopt a child. "I have to do it," she said. "I'm getting older. I want to share so many things. I want to shop, buy her little clothes and teach her the stock market."[13]

Oprah Winfrey

Oprah Winfrey

If She Can Make It . . .

The 15 million Americans who watch her talk show every day know that Oprah Winfrey is smart, funny, sincere, and concerned about other people.[1] Few people, however, may realize that she is also a very savvy businessperson. Winfrey not only is the star of her talk show but also the owner. That means she receives a substantial percentage of the show's profits. She also owns a production company and a studio. Today, Winfrey is worth about $250 million and is America's highest-paid entertainer.[2] That is quite an accomplishment for an African-American woman who endured abuse and poverty, among other hardships.

Curiously, Winfrey also has faced criticism because of her success. "A small but vocal group of black people fear me," she has said. "A black person has to ask herself, 'If Oprah Winfrey can make it, what does it say about me?' They no longer have any excuses."[3]

Oprah Gail Winfrey was born on January 29, 1954, in Kosciusko, Mississippi. She was supposed to be named Orpah, after the Bible figure. However, her name was misspelled on the birth certificate as "Oprah."

Oprah's mother, Vernita Lee, and father, Vernon Winfrey, were never married. Shortly after Oprah's birth, Vernita Lee moved to Milwaukee, Wisconsin. She left the baby with her mother in Mississippi. Vernon Winfrey, who was in the Army, returned to his post at Fort Rucker, Alabama.

Oprah's grandmother was very poor. She was unable to buy toys, or even shoes, for the little girl. The house had no running water or bathroom. "I never saw a movie, and maybe twice a year I got to see somebody's television," Oprah said.[4]

When Oprah was six, she went to live with her mother and two half-brothers in Milwaukee, Wisconsin. Her mother struggled to make ends meet. After awhile, the young girl moved in with her father. He had gotten married and was by then living in Nashville, Tennessee.

For the next eight years, Oprah bounced back and forth between homes. As a teenager, she began getting into trouble. It was also during this time that

Oprah was sexually abused by male family members.[5]

In 1968, Oprah went to live with Vernon Winfrey permanently. Winfrey said years later:

> I was definitely headed for a career as a juvenile delinquent. When my father took me, it changed the course of my life. He saved me. He simply knew what he wanted and expected. He would take nothing less.[6]

With Vernon Winfrey, Oprah found the discipline and attention she craved. She excelled in school and became involved in extracurricular activities. When she was sixteen, she was voted most popular girl in her class. Two years later, during her senior year, Oprah was elected president of the high-school student council.

Oprah also began entering beauty pageants. In 1971, she won the title of Miss Fire Prevention in Nashville. This contest was sponsored by Nashville radio station WVOL. When Oprah went to the radio station to collect her prizes, she met one of the producers. He liked her voice and hired her to read the news part-time after school. This was Oprah's first broadcasting experience.

In 1972, Oprah Winfrey enrolled at Tennessee State University, an all-black college in Nashville. Though she had won a four-year scholarship in a beauty pageant, she was eager to work. During her sophomore year, Winfrey became a part-time reporter on WTVF-TV, a CBS station. She was the youngest woman and the first African-American newscaster in Nashville. "[I was] the only news anchor in the country who had to be home by midnight," she said.[7]

Winfrey became a full-time news anchor after she graduated from college in 1976. Eager for adventure, however, she decided to leave Nashville. She quickly landed a news job at WJZ-TV, an ABC affiliate in Baltimore.

Winfrey was hired to co-anchor the 6:00 P.M. newscast, but she did not succeed. It was too difficult for her to keep her emotions hidden and remain objective, as reporters are supposed to do. After a year, she received a new assignment, to cohost *People Are Talking*. On this morning talk show, Winfrey was able to let her personality shine through. "This is what I was born to do," Winfrey said. "This is like breathing."[8] The program became very popular.

In 1984, Winfrey moved to Chicago to host another talk show. *AM Chicago* was doing poorly in the ratings. Its competition was *The Phil Donahue Show*. This was a local talk show that had done so well, it became syndicated. When a show is syndicated, television stations in other parts of the country pay money for the right to broadcast it.

No one expected Winfrey to beat Phil Donahue in the Chicago ratings. But with her on board, *AM Chicago* was an instant hit. Soon, the show was expanded from a half-hour to an hour. It was renamed *The Oprah Winfrey Show*.

Oprah Winfrey became the popular hostess of her own talk show, *The Oprah Winfrey Show*, in 1984.

Like other daytime programs, Winfrey's show tackled controversial topics such as racial discrimination, homosexuality, and child abuse. What made Winfrey unique, however, is that she was not merely a moderator during these discussions. Instead, she revealed her feelings and past experiences. Winfrey has candidly discussed her weight problems and dependency on men, among other things.

"Nobody was talking about their own problems like Oprah," said fellow talk-show host Maury Povich. "Talk-show hosts didn't talk about themselves. Oprah opened up a lot of new windows for viewers because they could empathize with her."[9]

In 1986, it was Winfrey's turn for syndication. Her show "became, quite simply, the hottest, most lucrative talk show in the country," *Ladies Home Journal* magazine reported.[10] Today, *The Oprah Winfrey Show* is the top-rated talk show in the history of television.[11] It is broadcast in about two hundred television markets and twelve foreign countries. It also has won several awards for best talk show. Winfrey herself has won awards for best talk-show host.

In August 1986, Winfrey formed Harpo ("Oprah" spelled backward) Productions to produce her talk show as well as films, videos, and television movies. One of Harpo's projects was producing Winfrey's prime-time special with singer Michael Jackson in 1993. That show became one of the most watched entertainment programs in history.

The Oprah Winfrey Show is the top-rated show in the history of television. Here, Winfrey chats with an audience member.

Harpo Productions is housed in a huge studio that Winfrey had built in Chicago. She is the first African American, and only the third woman in history, to own her own television studio.[12] Owning the studio that produces her program enables Winfrey to have more control over her schedule. She also is better able to oversee marketing, production, and other details.

Today, Winfrey employs more than one hundred men and women who work on her talk show and other projects. She is considered a demanding but generous boss. "I don't want anybody working for me who isn't happy at their job," she has said.[13]

Typically, Winfrey arrives at the office each day by 6:00 A.M. She exercises, studies notes for that day's shows, and tapes two programs. Then she holds staff meetings and completes paperwork. Often she does not leave for home until 9 P.M.

It is a grueling schedule, but Winfrey is well-compensated financially. She owns a condominium in Chicago as well as a 160-acre farm in Indiana. She also dresses in expensive designer clothes. Yet Winfrey also gives a lot of money to charities.

Winfrey also has invested her money in other ventures. She is part-owner of three television stations. She also co-owns a restaurant in Chicago.

So what is next for America's hottest talk-show host? Winfrey is likely to appear in more movies and television dramas. She was nominated for an

Academy Award for her first movie role, as Sofia, in 1985's *The Color Purple.*

Winfrey also may become more involved in national issues. She helped write legislation to create a national data bank for sex offenders. In fact, in its December 5, 1994, issue, *Time* magazine named Winfrey as one of fifty future leaders who will help shape American society.

Then there is her long-anticipated, but so far unscheduled, marriage to Stedman Graham, her steady boyfriend of several years. Winfrey said in 1993:

> I am in no hurry to get married. I dislike this notion of a desperate woman who wants to get married. The only reason to get married is to have children, and I don't feel the urgency. All the shows I've done on marriages give me more cause to examine it.[14]

No matter what lies ahead, Winfrey is confident, and happy. "I have a sense of greatness which comes from feeling that I'm doing what I'm supposed to be doing on the planet—empowering people, especially women," she said.[15] She added, "I am so grateful for my life. I wouldn't trade my life with anyone."[16]

Debbi Fields

Debbi Fields

Sweet Smell, and Taste, of Success

Success has been sweet for Debbi Fields—in more ways than one. The former homemaker turned a love of chocolate into Mrs. Fields, a gourmet cookie store. It became so popular that Debbi opened another store, and then another. In just eleven years, she ran more than five hundred Mrs. Fields stores in the United States and five other countries.

Fields' quick success was almost her downfall, however. Her company grew so big, and so fast, that she began to lose control of it. Yet Fields remained upbeat and took action to put her company back on the right track. Today, Mrs. Fields, Inc., is strong again. Debbi Fields has said:

> [Success] can take a long, long time, but it will never come from scheming or wishing or

doing somebody else's dance. If you do what you love to do, and do it as well as you know in your heart you can, it will eventually show up. When you least expect it. When, often enough, you've given up all hope of it ever arriving.[1]

Debra Jane Sivyer was born on September 18, 1956, in East Oakland, California. She was the youngest of four daughters of Edwin Sivyer, a civilian welder for the United States Navy, and Mary Sivyer, a homemaker. Debbi was an athletic and mischievous child. Her grades were average, but her traditional parents were not concerned. They believed it was more important for girls to learn how to cook and keep house.[2]

Debbi did not have many friends when she was growing up. "I refused to go along with the crowd," she recalled. "If everybody had to have a certain kind of shirt, I didn't want it. If everybody was going to a wild party, I refused to go. I just wanted to be different."[3]

Debbi did have one close friend, named Wendi. The two girls shared a love of chocolate, so Debbi often made chocolate chip cookies. At first, Debbi simply followed the recipe on the Toll House® chocolate chip package. Then she began experimenting. By the time she was thirteen, Debbi had developed her own recipe. It would one day be known as the Mrs. Fields chocolate chip cookie recipe.

At thirteen, Debbi also began working part-time for pocket money. Her parents were not poor, but there was little money to spare. "I learned early in life that if I wanted to have something, I had to work for it," Debbi recalled.[4] Her first job was catching foul balls for the Oakland A's baseball team. When she was fifteen, she worked at a department store in the afternoons and on weekends.

Debbi graduated from high school in 1973. She did not want to go to college, but she was unsure what to do next. She spent a few months in Lake Tahoe, Nevada, skiing and working as a nanny. Then she returned to Oakland. She continued to ski as often as she could. She worked part-time in department stores to pay for her hobby. She also took some courses at Los Altos Community College, near her family's home.

On one ski trip to Denver, Debbi was stranded at the airport because of bad weather. As she was making a telephone call, an older man came up and introduced himself. He was Randy Fields, an economist who had his own financial management business. Like Debbi, he was a Californian and an avid skier. The two began talking and quickly fell in love. After only a few months, they were married. Debbi was only eighteen years old, and Randy was twenty-eight.

The newlyweds settled in Menlo Park, California. Randy Fields was very busy with his career. Debbi Fields often felt inferior to her intelligent husband and his colleagues.[5] She was restless and anxious to strike out on her own. "I needed to share

95

something of myself with the world," she recalled. "I wanted to give, to be part of things. I just wasn't ready to become invisible—a nonparticipant [in life]."[6]

Fields began thinking about opening a store to sell her chocolate chip cookies. She had been making batches for Randy to take to his business meetings. His clients loved them. In fact, they often specifically requested them. Debbi Fields was confident that others would enjoy, and be willing to pay for, her cookies. They were bigger than those that could be purchased at grocery stores or bakeries. They also contained a lot more chips. Fields used only the finest ingredients to ensure they tasted delicious.

Fields' idea was to open a store that served the cookies soft, warm, and fresh, "as though you'd stopped by my house and caught me just taking a batch from the oven," she said.[7] She asked other people for advice. Few, however, were enthusiastic about the business venture. They did not think people would be willing to pay for something they could easily bake at home. Also, studies had shown that consumers preferred crispy, not soft, cookies.

Fields was undeterred. With Randy's aid, she borrowed some money from a banker who was a big fan of her cookies. She also borrowed money from Randy. Then Debbi found space to rent in a shopping arcade in Palo Alto, California. She purchased commercial baking ovens, sinks, and other equipment. Finally, she arranged to receive supplies of chocolate and other ingredients.

Debbi Fields' first day of business was August 18, 1977. She was only twenty years old. She arrived at the store at 6:00 A.M. to start baking for the 9:00 A.M. opening. By noon, however, she had not sold a single cookie.

Fields piled the cookies on a tray and began walking outside the arcade. She handed out free samples. With a big smile on her face, she encouraged tasters to stop by her store and buy some cookies to take home. By the end of the day, Fields had earned $50.

Fields' store soon became very popular. In 1979, she opened a second location, in San Francisco. Fields had not planned on expanding her business. However, the builder of the San Francisco mall was a customer of hers. He convinced Fields that she would find appreciative customers in the new mall as well. "I certainly didn't have the vision that we could go beyond one [location]," she recalled.[8] On that store's opening day, customers waited for Fields' cookies in a line that wrapped around the block.

Debbi and Randy's daughter, Jessica, was born in 1979. Two years later, daughter Jenessa was born. By the end of 1981, Debbi had fourteen Mrs. Fields stores. She moved the company's headquarters to the ski resort of Park City, Utah. A few years later, Randy became chief financial officer of Mrs. Fields, Inc. Debbi remained president and chief executive officer.

The next few years were very busy for Fields, personally as well as professionally. Another daughter, Jennifer, was born in 1984. By the time daughter Ashley came along in 1988, Fields had more than five hundred stores in the United States, Japan, and Australia. A fifth daughter, McKenzie, was born in 1991.

Debbi Fields was very involved with her business, which was earning millions of dollars. When she was not creating new recipes, she was visiting her stores. Workers came to know Fields as an outgoing and friendly leader with very strict standards. If cookies came out of the oven too flat or even slightly overcooked, Fields' rule was to throw them away. Any cookie not sold two hours after it was baked was given to charitable groups. One time, Fields taste-tested eight hundred brownies in a single day, trying to perfect the recipe.

As much as she enjoyed her work, however, Fields learned she could not do it all. She became so involved with little details that she did not have time to plan for her company's future. Other gourmet cookie companies soon came on the market, and Mrs. Fields foundered.

Debbi Fields learned to delegate. She hired a team of executives to share her responsibilities. That gave her more time to plan for the future:

> In the past I used to ask [store] managers what they needed, and then I did it for them. "Your ice machine is broken? Your milk

delivery is off? I'll take care of it." If I saw something I didn't like, I fixed it myself, right then and there. Those days are over. Now I literally have to stop myself. Letting go has been hard.[9]

She added, "I have worked very hard on removing myself from the day-to-day details that do not allow me to keep the company focused on where it's going."[10]

Today, Mrs. Fields stores continue to serve Fields' original chocolate chip cookies. They also offer brownies and other sweet treats. Fields has about six hundred stores in the United States and six other countries. This figure includes Mrs. Fields stores in more than one hundred highway toll plazas. Mrs. Fields bakery-cafes offer soup and sandwiches along with desserts.

Juggling motherhood with a successful business has been tricky, Fields admits. One way she coped was involving her daughters with her business:

> The one thing I have done is make sure the kids really understood what Mom does. They are very involved. For the summer, for example, I've given the girls cookie projects to work on. I have created the ideas, but the girls actually work on some of my recipes at home, and they think it's fun. So I'm keeping them busy . . . but they also are involved in the business in some small way, which is very important to me.[11]

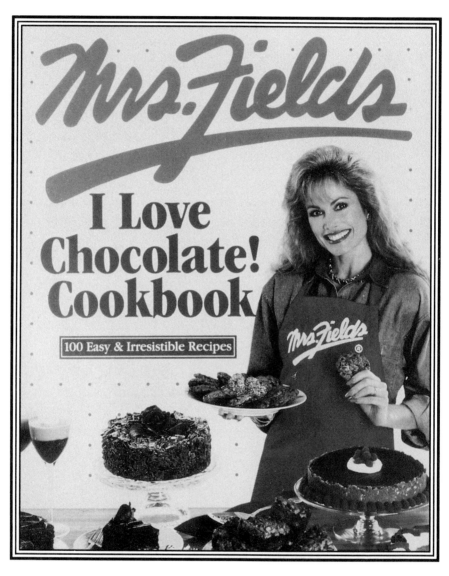

Debbi Fields is also the author of the *Mrs. Fields "I Love Chocolate!" Cookbook.*

Debbi Fields had few supporters when she had the idea to open her first cookie store. Now, as a successful entrepreneur, she wants to encourage others. She offers this advice to people interested in owning their own business:

> You must never be afraid of failure. . . . You will find more people in the world who will tell you that you can't do it than who will tell you that you can. . . . Believe in what you are doing. The word 'no' is completely unacceptable. . . . You have to have fun! Otherwise, life is like one long dental appointment.[12]

Chapter Notes

Preface

1. Associated Press, "Daughters Succeed Mothers as Owners of Small Businesses," *Richmond Times-Dispatch*, February 6, 1995, p. D15.

2. Ibid.

3. Anne B. Fisher, "When Will Women Get to the Top," *Fortune*, September 21, 1992, p. 44.

4. Current Population Survey, United States Department of Labor, Bureau of Labor Statistics, 1994.

Chapter 1

1. Caroline Bird, *Enterprising Women* (New York: Norton, 1976), p. 169.

2. "Maggie L. Walker National Historic Site: An Orientation," prepared by Celia Jackson Suggs, p. 4.

3. Ibid.

4. Biographical sketch of Maggie Walker, provided to United States Maritime Commission by Right Worthy Grand Council Independent Order of Saint Luke (no date).

5. Bird, p. 170.

6. "Richmonder Honored for Her True Work," letter to editor of the *Richmond News Leader*, 1934 (no exact date).

7. Wendell P. Dabney, *Maggie L. Walker, Her Life and Deeds* (Cincinnati, Ohio: Dabney, 1927), p. 117.

Chapter 2

1. Jessie Carney Smith, ed., *Notable Black American Women* (Detroit: Gale Research, 1991), p. 1185.

2. Ibid.

3. A'Lelia Perry Bundles, *Madam C. J. Walker: Entrepreneur* (New York: Chelsea House, 1991), p. 61.

4. Caroline Bird, *Enterprising Women* (New York: Norton, 1976), p. 130.

5. Bundles, p. 61.

6. Smith, p. 1187.

7. Bundles, p. 63.

Chapter 3

1. Peter Wyden, "Danger: Boss Lady at Work," *Saturday Evening Post*, August 8, 1959, p. 27.

2. Ibid.

3. Biography of Olive Ann Beech, chairman emeritus, Beech Aircraft Corporation, provided by Beech Aircraft Corporation, pp. 2–3 (undated).

4. Arthur M. Louis, "The Hall of Fame for U.S. Business Leadership," *Fortune*, April 4, 1983, p. 145.

5. "Beechcraft Takes Off on the Wings of a Jet," *Business Week*, February 25, 1956, p. 180.

6. Ibid., p. 184.

7. "Olive Ann Can Handle This," *Fortune*, May 1947, p. 146.

8. "A Job for Olive Ann," *Time*, December 25, 1950, p. 54.

9. "Mrs. O. A. Beech Dies at Age 89," *The Beechcrafter: A Publication About Beech Aircraft Corporation*, July 6, 1993, p. 2.

Chapter 4

1. "Ruth Handler: Barbie's Mom," press release provided by Mattel, Inc.

2. Wyndham Robertson, "The Ten Highest-Ranking Women in Big Business," *Fortune*, April 1973, p. 87.

3. Frank J. Taylor, "Million-Dollar Music Box," *Saturday Evening Post*, December 6, 1952, p. 113.

4. Ibid.

5. Ruth Handler with Jacqueline Shannon, *Dream Doll: The Ruth Handler Story* (Stamford, Conn.: Longmeadow Press, 1994), p. 60.

6. Taylor, p. 29.

7. Robertson, p. 87.

8. Handler and Shannon, p. 8.

9. Ibid., p. 9.

10. Ibid., p. 107.

11. Lisa Miller Mesdag, "From Barbie Dolls to Real Life," *Fortune*, September 8, 1980, p. 88.

12. Handler and Shannon, p. 121.

Chapter 5

1. Carol Felsenthal, *Power, Privilege and the Post: The Katharine Graham Story* (New York: Putnam, 1993), p. 156.

2. Jean Stafford, "Katharine Graham," *Vogue*, December 1973, p. 218.

3. Felsenthal, p. 39.

4. Susanna McBee, "Katharine Graham and How She Grew," *McCalls*, September 1971, p. 79.

5. "Guest at Breakfast," *Time*, April 16, 1956, p. 70.

6. Deborah Davis, *Katharine the Great: Katharine Graham and Her Washington Post Empire* (New York: Sheridan Square Press, 1991), p. 72.

7. McBee, p. 134.

8. Felsenthal, p. 111.

9. Ibid., p. 157.

10. Ibid., p. 228.

11. Davis, p. 184.

12. Donald Robinson, *The 100 Most Important People in the World Today* (New York: Putnam, 1970), p. 175.

13. Felsenthal, p. 450.

Chapter 6

1. Phyllis Battelle, "Eileen Ford, 'How I Find Those Fabulous Faces,'" *Good Housekeeping,* June 1982, p. 145.

2. Ibid.

3. "When I Was Sixteen," *Good Housekeeping,* October 1968, p. 101.

4. Ibid.

5. "Eileen Ford," *Current Biography Yearbook 1971,* (New York: H.W. Wilson Co., 1972), p. 136.

6. Judy Bachrach, "Eileen Ford: Critics Say She Sees Only Blond, But When Push Comes to Shove, She's Still Queen of the Skin Trade," *People,* May 16, 1983, p. 105.

7. "Family-Style Model Agency," *Life,* October 4, 1948, p. 63.

8. Scott Cohen, *Meet the Makers: The People Behind the Product* (New York: St. Martin's Press, 1979), p. 74.

9. "The Business of Being Beautiful," *Harper's Bazaar,* January 1979, p. 94.

10. James Mills, "The Godmother," *Life,* November 13, 1970, p. 68.

11. Battelle, pp. 143–144.

12. Cohen, p. 77.

13. Mills, p. 78.

Chapter 7

1. Nelda LaTeef, *Working Women for the 21st Century: Fifty Women Reveal Their Pathways to Success* (Charlotte, Vt.: Williamson, 1992), p. 58.

2. Molly Broughton Peter, "Washington Report: The Three Women in Washington with the Most Clout," *Glamour,* August 1980, p. 92.

3. "Alice Rivlin," in *Current Biography Yearbook 1982* (New York: H.W. Wilson Co., 1983) p. 356.

4. Ibid., p. 357.

5. "Everyone's Wild Over Alice," *Time,* July 18, 1977, p. 71.

6. Ibid., pp. 67, 71.

7. Adam Smith, "Alice and Bill and the Struggles at Budget Gap," *Esquire,* July 1984, p. 87.

8. Suneel Ratan, "Shifting Power Out Of The Beltway," *Fortune,* June 29, 1992, p. 25.

9. Ibid., p. 26.

10. Michael Kramer, "Clinton's Identity Crisis," *Time,* November 7, 1994, p. 39.

11. Marshall Loeb, "Her Hand is On The Future," *Time,* June 18, 1979, p. 58.

12. LaTeef, p. 59.

13. Ibid., p. 60.

Chapter 8

1. Christopher Knowlton, "Wall Street Finds A Million-Dollar Oracle at Shearson," *Fortune,* January 4, 1988, p. 28.

2. Susan Antilla, "The Hottest Woman on Wall Street," *Working Woman,* August 1991, p. 51.

3. Knowlton, p. 28.

4. Joseph Nocera, "Nice Call, Guys," *Esquire,* October 1989, p. 79.

5. Greg Anrig, Jr., "Money Profile: The Newest Seer Now Predicts a Bear Market Rally (What A Relief!)," *Money,* December 1987, p. 232.

6. Nancy Hass, "The Guru Is Gloomy Again," *Newsweek,* March 28, 1994, p. 40.

7. Kathleen Davis, "Springfield's Elaine Garzarelli: She's Number One on Wall Street," *Springfield Press,* August 26, 1987, p. 1.

8. Nocera, p. 81.

9. John Greenwald, "Where's Garzarelli Going?" *Time*, November 7, 1994, p. 59.

10. Fred Tasker, "Wall Street Maverick Does It Her Way," *Miami Herald*, April 23, 1995, p. 1J.

11. Ibid., p. 8J.

12. Ibid.

13. Antilla, p. 51.

Chapter 9

1. Paul Noglows, "Oprah: The Year of Living Dangerously," *Working Woman*, May 1994, p. 52.

2. Ibid.

3. Barbara Grizzuti Harrison, "The Importance of Being Oprah," *New York Times Magazine*, June 11, 1989, p. 130.

4. Norman King, *Everybody Loves Oprah!: Her Remarkable Life Story* (New York: Morrow, 1987), p. 34.

5. Jill Brooke Coiner, "Oprah Sets the Record Straight," *McCalls*, November 1993, p. 149.

6. King, pp. 56, 58.

7. "Oprah Winfrey," in *Current Biography Yearbook 1987* (New York: H.W. Wilson Co., 1988), p. 611.

8. Ibid., p. 612.

9. Noglows, p. 54.

10. Miriam Kanner, "Oprah at 40: What She's Learned the Hard Way," *Ladies Home Journal*, February 1994, p. 99.

11. Fred Goodman, "Madonna and Oprah: The Companies They Keep," *Working Woman*, December 1991, p. 54.

12. Noglows, p. 52.

13. Goodman, p. 55.

14. Coiner, p. 148.

15. Kanner, p. 166.

16. Coiner, p. 201.

Chapter 10

1. Debbi Fields and Alan Furst, *One Smart Cookie* (New York: Simon and Schuster, 1987), p. 83.

2. Ibid.

3. Ibid., p. 21.

4. Alan Furst, "The Golden Age of Goo: How Debbi and Randy Fields Unleashed a Cookie Monster," *Esquire*, December 1984, p. 326.

5. Fields and Furst, p. 56.

6. Ibid.

7. Ibid., p. 80.

8. Nelda LaTeef, *Working Women for the 21st Century: Fifty Women Reveal Their Pathways to Success* (Charlotte, Vt.: Williamson, 1992), p. 64.

9. Alan Prendergast, "Learning to Let Go: Holding on Too Tight Almost Made the Cookie Crumble at Mrs. Fields," *Working Woman*, January 1992, p. 42.

10. Katherine Weisman, "Succeeding by Failing," *Forbes*, June 25, 1990, p. 160.

11. LaTeef, p. 64.

12. "What She Forgot," *Nation's Business*, April 1986, p. 21.

Index

A

AM Chicago, 86
Augusta, Kansas, 28
Aviation Hall of Fame, 34

B

Baltimore, Maryland, 11, 86
Barbie®, 37, 41-43
Barnard College, 58
Beech Aircraft Corporation,
   27, 30, 31, 33, 34
Beech, Mary Lynn, 31
Beech, Olive Ann, 5, 27-35
Beech, Suzanne, 31
Beech, Walter, 29, 30, 31, 33
Bendix Transcontinental
   Speed Dash, 31
Bernstein, Carl, 54
Black Monday, 79
Bloomington, Indiana, 66
Boca Raton, Florida, 81
Bradlee, Benjamin, 52
Breedlove, Alex, 18
Breedlove, Louvenia, 18
Breedlove, Minerva, 18
Breedlove, Owen, 18
Breedlove, Sarah. *See* Walker,
   Madam C.J.
Brookings Institution, 67, 69
Bryn Mawr College, 66
Bryn Mawr, Pennsylvania, 66

C

Cambridge, Massachusetts, 66
Carter, Jimmy, 69
Chicago, Illinois, 22, 86, 90
Civil War, 4, 10, 17
Clinton, Bill, 6, 65, 70, 72
Color Purple, The, 91

Congressional Budget Office,
   68-69
Consolidated Bank and Trust
   Company, The, 13
Cuthbert, Eccles, 10

D

Delta, Louisiana, 18
Denver, Colorado, 18, 20, 22,
   37, 38, 95
Draper, Elizabeth, 10
Drexel University, 76

E

East Oakland, California, 94,
   95
Eisenhower, Dwight, 34-35

F

Fields, Ashley, 98
Fields, Debbi, 6, 93-101
Fields, Jenessa, 97
Fields, Jennifer, 98
Fields, Jessica, 97
Fields, McKenzie, 98
Fields, Randy, 95, 96, 97
Ford, Bill, 60
Ford, Eileen, 5, 57-63
Ford, Jamie, 59
Ford, Jerry, 58-59, 60, 61
Ford, Katie, 60
Ford, Lacey, 60
Fort Rucker, Alabama, 84

G

Garzarelli Capital, 81
Garzarelli, Elaine, 6, 75-81
Garzarelli, Ida, 76
Garzarelli, Ralph, 75, 79
Garzarelli, Robert, 76, 79
glass ceiling, 45

Glossine, 20, 21
Graham, Donald, 50, 54
Graham, Elizabeth, 50
Graham, Katharine, 5, 47-55
Graham, Philip, 47, 49, 50, 51
Graham, Stedman, 91
Graham, Stephen, 51
Graham, William, 51
Great Depression, 13, 30
Great Neck, New York, 58

H
Handler, Barbara, 40, 45
Handler, Elliot, 38, 39, 40,
    41, 43, 45
Handler, Ken, 40, 45
Handler, Ruth, 5, 37-45
Harpo Productions, 88, 90
Harvard University, 70
Hedrick, Frank E., 34

I
Independent Order of Saint
    Luke, 10-11, 12, 15
Indianapolis, Indiana, 21
Institutional Investor, 77
Irvington-on-Hudson, New
    York, 22

J
Johnson, Lyndon B., 35, 67

K
Knoxville College, 20
Korean War, 33
Kosciusko, Mississippi, 84

L
Lake Tahoe, Nevada, 95
Lelia College, 21
Los Altos Community
    College, 95
Los Angeles, California, 22,
    38, 39

M
MacArthur Foundation, 69
Matson, Harold, 40
Mattel, Inc., 5, 37, 40-41, 43
McWilliams, Moses, 18
Mellor, Frank, 28
Mellor, Suzannah, 28
Menlo Park, California, 95
Meyer, Agnes, 47, 48
Meyer, Eugene, 47, 48, 49, 50
Milwaukee, Wisconsin, 84
Mitchell, Allan, 65
Mitchell, Georgianna, 65
Mitchell, William, 10
Moor, Roy E., 76, 77
Mosko, Ida, 38
Mosko, Jacob, 37
Mosko, Joe, 38
Mosko, Sarah, 38, 39, 40
Mrs. Fields, Inc., 6, 93, 96-99

N
Nashville, Tennessee, 84, 85, 86
National Aeronautics and
    Space Administration
    (NASA), 33
National Aeronautics
    Association, 34
National Association for the
    Advancement of Colored
    People (NAACP), 15, 24
Nearly Me, 43, 45
Newsweek, 51, 54
New York City, New York,
    22, 48, 58
Nixon, Richard M., 5, 35, 54,
    67-68

O
Oprah Winfrey Show, The,
    86-89
Otte, Loretta, 58
Otte, Nathaniel, 58

P

Palo Alto, California, 96
Paramount Studios, 39
Park City, Utah, 97
Pentagon Papers, 52
People Are Talking, 86
Persian Gulf crisis, 79
Philadelphia, Pennsylvania, 65, 76
Phil Donahue Show, The, 86
Pittsburgh, Pennsylvania, 21
Poughkeepsie, New York, 49
Pulitzer Prize, 5, 54

R

Radcliffe College, 66
Reviving the American Dream, 70
Richmond, Virginia, 10
Rivlin, Alice, 6, 65-73
Rivlin, Lewis A., 66

S

Saint Louis, Missouri, 19, 24
Saint Luke Penny Savings Bank, 12, 13
San Francisco, California, 97
San Francisco News, 49
Sivyer, Edwin, 94
Sivyer, Mary, 94
Springfield, Pennsylvania, 75
St. Luke Herald, 12, 15

T

Tennessee State University, 85, 86
Times Herald, 50
Toy Industry Hall of Fame, 43
Travel Air Manufacturing, 28-29

Tuskegee, Alabama, 24-25
Tuskegee Institute, 19

U

University of Chicago, 49
University of Denver, 38
University of Indiana, 66

V

Van Lew, Elizabeth, 10
Vassar College, 49
Vegetable Shampoo, 20, 21
Vicksburg, Mississippi, 18
Vietnam, 52

W

Walker, A'Lelia, 18, 19, 20, 21, 22, 24
Walker, Armstead, 11, 13
Walker, Charles Joseph, 20, 22
Walker, Madam C.J., 4, 17-25
Walker, Maggie L., 6, 9-15
Walker, Melvin, 11
Walker, Russell, 11, 13
Washington, Booker T., 19
Washington, D.C., 48, 49, 66
Washington, Margaret, 19
Washington Post, The, 5, 47, 48-54, 72
Watergate, 5, 54
Waverly, Kansas, 27
Wichita, Kansas, 28, 30, 35
Winfrey, Oprah, 5, 83-91
Winfrey, Vernon, 84, 85
Wonderful Hair Grower, 20, 21
Woodward, Bob, 54
World's Fair of 1904, 19
World War II, 31-33, 50